Creative Homework Assignments
Engaging Take-Home Activities
That Reinforce Basic Skills

Grades 2–3

by Linda De Geronimo
and Anne Diehl

Carson-Dellosa Publishing Company, Inc.
Greensboro, North Carolina

Credits

Editors: Kelly Morris Huxmann, Joey Bland
Layout Design: Van Harris
Inside Illustrations: Phyllis Harris
Cover Design: Van Harris
Cover Illustration: Phyllis Harris

Printed in the USA • All rights reserved.   ISBN 978-159441-362-9

Table of Contents

SCIENCE & HEALTH TASK CARDS

SOCIAL STUDIES TASK CARDS

Introduction

A teacher in a typical school district is required to assign homework at least four times per week. Traditional homework assignments usually offer practice or reinforcement of content addressed in class, and can include memorizing math facts or spelling words, or studying at home to prepare for a test. Have you ever been troubled by your students' lack of enthusiasm when you assign such tasks? If so, it's time to break up the routine and challenge your students with *Creative Homework Assignments*.

Divided by curriculum area, this book offers more than 140 unique ideas for homework activities. Each activity page contains two task cards designed to be copied and attached to 5" x 8" (13 cm x 20 cm) index cards or card stock. The task cards include activities that can be sent home with students at any time of the year. For some activities (like pages 12, 17, and 28), you may need to fill in information on the card before sending it home with the students; however, most cards are ready to send as is. Select the activities that best suit your needs and the needs of your students.

The activities can be used for additional practice of familiar skills or as enrichment activities; they can be quick assignments that are due the next day or can be extended over a longer period of time—it is your choice. Since your students will be actively involved as they examine information, analyze data, solve problems, design products, make evaluations and choices, and apply past knowledge, you will be helping them develop critical thinking skills. You will also provide students and their families with opportunities to interact as they work together on the projects and activities.

For your convenience, a sample parent/guardian letter (page 7) and homework supply list (page 8) are included to help inform parents about the task cards you will be sending home. The letter contains advice for parents about providing a quiet homework nook for children, and the supply list will help them prepare for upcoming projects. For some activities, you may elect to send certain supplies home with your students. Before completing any food activity, ask families' permission, and inquire about students' food allergies and religious or other food preferences. Encourage substitutions where appropriate.

After using the activities in *Creative Homework Assignments* a few times, you shouldn't hear as many groans from your students when you mention the word "homework." Instead, you'll hear, "What's for homework tonight?"

Dear Parent/Guardian,

I am delighted to have your child in my class this year. We will be working very hard together on reading, writing, and math skills, and will be involved in many activities related to other areas of the curriculum, such as science, health, and social studies. Your child will also be learning important social skills while interacting with classmates.

Throughout the year, your child will be bringing home task cards that will require your guidance. These cards are designed to support and enhance our standards-based curriculum. The tasks on the cards are meant to be fun and engaging, and they will require more than just rote practice or memorization to complete. The activities will help your child develop critical thinking skills. Your child may be asked to examine information, analyze data, solve problems, design products, make evaluations or choices, and apply past knowledge.

Your guidance in some of the activities will provide a great opportunity to spend quality time with your child, as well as benefit your child's academic and social growth. As each task is accomplished, you will learn more about your child's strengths and weaknesses. You will discover which activities may require additional practice as the year progresses.

Each task card your child brings home will have a due date listed. Activities will not necessarily need to be completed in one night. In addition, some materials required to complete an activity may be sent home with your child. You may need to provide other simple items, such as dry cereal, flour, glue, or tape. Attached is a list of supplies your child may need to complete some homework assignments. These items will most likely be needed to accomplish other school projects as well. Help your child create a homework nook at home and store the supplies in this special place. This will help your child get organized and save time when working on assignments.

The activities on the task cards should prove to be fun for your child and other members of the family. I hope that you will enjoy helping your child complete these special tasks and watching him/her develop higher-level thinking skills as he/she uses important skills in all areas of our curriculum.

Please feel free to contact me with any questions and concerns. Your feedback as a partner in your child's education is important, and is always welcomed and appreciated.

Sincerely,

Homework Supply List

Help create a homework nook at home for your child. Then, gather the following supplies and keep them in this special work space. You will find that your child uses these basic supplies again and again for school projects and assignments. The additional supplies may only be needed for a limited number of activities.

Basic Supplies

3" x 5" (8 cm x 13 cm) small index cards
5" x 8" (13 cm x 20 cm) large index cards
construction paper (assorted colors)
writing paper
notebooks
pencils
pens
crayons
markers
scissors
glue sticks
stapler
tape
craft sticks
ribbon, yarn, and string
buttons, glitter, and feathers
fabric scraps
paper plates
paper bags (large and small)
small paper cups or clear plastic cups
calculator
clocks (digital and analog)
dice
deck of playing cards
assortment of books and fairy tales
old magazines and newspapers

Additional Supplies

class teddy bear or other mascot
popcorn
raisins
toothpicks
mini marshmallows
assorted cereals
candy-covered chocolates, like M&M's®
clear plastic or glass jar with a lid
U.S. coins and dollar bills
socks
tortillas or square sandwich bread
mini pretzels
variety of dry pasta shapes
food coloring
resealable plastic bags
paper towels
ice-cube tray
bowl
recent photo
piggy bank
monthly calendar

Name: _____ Due Date: _____

Open House (Part 1)

Write a letter to your parent(s)/guardian(s). Invite them to attend your school's open house. Tell them why it is important for them to visit your classroom and meet with your teacher. Also, tell them what you think your teacher might say about your work and behavior in school.

Use the invitation from Part 2 to provide all of the details about the event. Decorate the invitation with pictures of things you use at school.

Name: _____ Due Date: _____

Open House (Part 2)

You're Invited to an Open House!

Date: _____ Time: _____

School: _____

Teacher's Name: _____

Room Number: _____

Name: _____   Due Date: _____

Letter People

Write the first letter of your first name in the middle of a piece of construction paper. Make the letter really big. Then, see if you can turn the letter into a person, an animal, or one of your favorite things. Look at the example on this card. Bring your picture to school to share with your classmates.

Try again with the first letter of your last name.

Name: _____   Due Date: _____

Name Poetry

Write your first name on a piece of paper. Make the letters go down the page instead of across. Then, write a phrase starting with each letter to describe yourself. This is called an **acrostic poem**. See the examples below for ideas.

A pretty girl   Best at baseball

Nice to pets   Easy to talk to

Neat and clean   Nice to his friends

Bring your finished poem to school to share with your classmates.

Name: _____   Due Date: _____

Teddy's Story (Part 1)

It is your turn to take the class teddy bear home for the night. Keep track of what you and Teddy do after school, before bedtime, and before school the next day. Draw pictures and take notes on this card to help you remember what you did. Tell Teddy's story to the class.

_____

_____

_____

_____

Name: _____   Due Date: _____

Teddy's Story (Part 2)

If Teddy could talk, what would he say about his visit to your home? What did he like best about his trip? What was his least favorite thing you did together? Be ready to tell Teddy's story to your classmates.

_____

_____

_____

_____

Name: _____ Due Date: _____

Show and Spell

Go on a search in your home. Look in the _____
for something that starts with the same letter as the name of that
room. For example, look in the den for something that starts with "d."

On the back of this card, write the name of what you found in uppercase
letters. Be sure the word is large enough for your classmates to read.

Bring the object (or a picture of it) to school. Keep the object hidden in
a bag and hold up this card. Have your classmates try to read the word
you wrote on the back. Then, show them the object to see if they read
the word correctly.

Name: _____ Due Date: _____

Label Your Home

Choose one room in your home.
Write the name of the room here: _____

Look around the room. Can you spell the names of the objects you see?
Pick 10 things in the room. Make labels for the objects with index cards.

Tape an index card to each thing. Close your eyes and practice spelling
each word in the room. When you can spell everything that is labeled,
draw a picture of the room on a large piece of paper. Include the 10
objects you named and label each one.

Try again. Make new cards for other things in the room.

Name: _____ Due Date: _____

Search for Blends

Some words begin with consonant blends, such as **ch, bl, cl, pl, fr, gr, tr, sp,** and **st**. Say the sound each blend makes. Then, choose one blend and search your home for things that start with that sound.

Draw a picture of each thing you find on the back of this card. Write the beginning blend at the top of the card.

How many things did you find? _____

Name: _____ Due Date: _____

Long Vowels

Write a vowel on each line below:

_____ _____ _____ _____ _____

When a vowel has a long sound, it says its name. Say each long vowel sound out loud. Then, choose one long vowel sound and search your home for things that have that sound. Write the long vowel on the back of this card. Then, draw a picture of each thing you find.

How many things did you find? _____

Name: _____ Due Date: _____

They Go Together

Write the name of something that goes with the first word in each phrase below.

left and _____   up and _____

comb and _____   milk and _____

table and _____   pencil and _____

salt and _____   run and _____

Name: _____ Due Date: _____

They Don't Go Together

Complete each phrase below with a word that does **not** belong.

left and _____   up and _____

comb and _____   milk and _____

table and _____   pencil and _____

salt and _____   run and _____

 CD-104158 Creative Homework Assignments

Name: _____ Due Date: _____

Dare to Compare

How are you the same as each thing below? How are you different?

	Same	Different
a car	_____	_____
a bear	_____	_____
your mom	_____	_____
your dad	_____	_____

Name: _____ Due Date: _____

Alike and Different

How is each set of things below alike? How are they different?
Use another piece of paper to record your answers.

a cat and a dog

a pencil and a pen

mittens and sandals

a piece of cheese and an apple

Name: _____ Due Date: _____

Fact or Fiction?

Read a book. As you read, see how many facts you can identify. A **fact** is something that is true. Next, see if you can find things that are made up. Something that is made up is called **fiction**. Look for three things that are fact and three things that are fiction. Write them below.

Fact	Fiction
_____	_____
_____	_____
_____	_____

Name: _____ Due Date: _____

Making Comparisons

Read two books about the same topic. The books can be fact or fiction. Compare information from the books using the Venn diagram below.

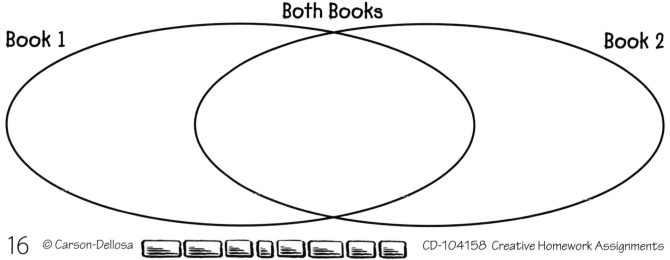

Both Books

Book 1   Book 2

 CD-104158 Creative Homework Assignments

Name: _____ Due Date: _____

Graphic Organizers

Use a graphic organizer to help list your thoughts before writing about a topic. Choose one of the organizers shown below or design your own.

Story Web

Story Map

Title: _____
Author: _____
Setting: _____
Characters: _____
_____
Beginning: _____
Middle: _____
End: _____

Chain Reaction

Name: _____ Due Date: _____

Webbing

A web can help you understand information about a topic. Here is an example of a web about dolphins.

bottlenose
spotted
spinner
buffeo
Types

oceans
rivers
pods
Live in

dorsal fin
flippers
beak
flukes
blowhole
Body features

Dolphins

fish
squid
crabs
shrimp
Eat

mammals
intelligent
Other facts

echolocation
clicks
whistles
Communicate with

Now create your own web.
Here is your topic: _____

Name: _____ Due Date: _____

Nouns and Verbs (Part 1)

A **noun** names a person, place, or thing. A **verb** is an action word.

Write each word from Part 2 on an index card. Then, sort the cards into two groups: nouns and verbs. Take one noun card and one verb card, and use them to make sentences. Ask an adult to read your sentences. Mix up the cards in each pile. Make more sentences by picking another card from each pile.

How many sentences did you make in all? _____
Write your favorite sentence on the line below.

_____

Name: _____ Due Date: _____

Nouns and Verbs (Part 2)

tree	baby	monkey	dentist	teacher
rainbow	rabbit	horse	woman	light
dog	frog	boy	sun	slept
cried	squealed	climbed	glowed	worked
talked	shined	faded	galloped	hopped
taught	crawled	barked	grabbed	ate

 CD-104158 Creative Homework Assignments

Name: _____ Due Date: _____

Action Words

Look at the list of words below. These words show action. They are called **verbs**.

hop   run   fly   walk   swim   crawl   jump

Choose one verb and circle it. Then, think of an animal that moves in that way. On the back of this card, draw a picture of the animal. Write the animal's name below your picture.

Practice moving like the animal you drew. Back at school, pretend to be your animal and let your classmates guess what you are.

Name: _____ Due Date: _____

Describe It

Find your favorite toy or animal at home. Look at it closely and think about words that you would use to describe it. You might use words like **huge, brown, furry, soft, hard, smart, tricky, fun,** or **fast.**

Pick five words to describe your favorite toy or animal. Write them below.

_____ _____ _____

_____ _____

Read the words to your classmates at school. Can they guess what you are describing?

Name: _____ Due Date: _____

Sharing Messages

Write a note to someone in your home. Tell about something special you did in school. Give the note to that person to read. Ask the person to write a message back about his or her own day. Use the space below to plan your note.

_____

_____

_____

_____

Name: _____ Due Date: _____

Be a Reporter

Find a picture that you like in a newspaper or a magazine. Tape or glue the picture to the back of this card. Then, ask an adult to tell you about the picture.

Practice retelling the same story. Bring the picture to school with you and tell the story to the class.

Name: _____ Due Date: _____

Guess Who I Am

Write a friendly letter to a classmate. Use "Dear Friend," as your greeting.

In the body of your letter, tell the person all about yourself. Be careful not to say your name or give specific clues that would tell someone who you are. For example, do not write, "I love to play with my brother Sam." Instead, say something like, "I love to play goalie on my soccer team."

For your closing, write "Guess who?"

Give your letter to the teacher, who will give it to one of your classmates. Did the classmate guess that you wrote the letter? _____

Name: _____ Due Date: _____

Who Are You?

Write a friendly letter to a classmate. Use "Dear Friend," as your greeting.

In the body of your letter, ask questions that will help you learn who the person is. Do not ask specific questions, like "What's your name?" Instead, ask something like "Do you play a sport?"

For your closing, write "Your friend," and sign your name so that you will get an answer to your letter.

Read the letter you receive carefully. Who do you think wrote it?

Write your guess here: _____

Name: _____ Due Date: _____

My School

Most children in the United States go to school five days a week for about six hours a day. School is a great place to learn and make new friends. Think about your own school. What do you like about it? What would you change about it if you could?

Write a letter to the principal of your school. Tell him or her all of the things you like about your school and some of the things you would like to change. Give your finished letter to the teacher, who will pass it on to the principal.

Name: _____ Due Date: _____

My Home

Home can be a great place. Think about your home. What do you like about it? What would you change about it if you could?

Write a letter to a friend. Tell your friend all of the things you like about your home and some of the things you would like to change.

Bring your letter to school to show your teacher. Then, give the letter to your friend.

Name: _____   Due Date: _____

What Am I?

Write your own "What Am I?" riddle. Look around your bedroom and list things that you see. Then, think of different ways you can describe one of the things you listed.

Example: I am soft and fluffy. You can lay your head
on me when you sleep. You can put a baby
tooth underneath me.
What am I?   (a pillow)

Try to write your own riddle about one of the items on your list. Then, try writing another riddle about a different item. Share your riddles in class.

Name: _____   Due Date: _____

Using Personification

Personification means describing an object as if it were a living thing. Try using personification to write a riddle.

Example: I can dance in the wind, in the trees,
or in the sky, but I have no legs.
What am I?   (a leaf)

Now, write your own riddle. Think of an object and try to describe it as if it were alive.

Name: _____   Due Date: _____

Make It Rhyme

Write a poem about your favorite holiday on the back of this card.
Your poem should have four lines total, and the second and fourth lines
should rhyme. To help you get started, try filling in the blank of the poem
below. Choose a word that rhymes with **year**.

My Birthday

My favorite day of all
Comes only once a year.
But, I don't mind the wait,
Because it's almost _____!

░░░░░░░░░░░░░░░░░░░░░░░░░░░░░░░░░

Name: _____   Due Date: _____

Make It Rhyme Again

Write a poem about your favorite sport on the back of this card.
Your poem should have four lines, and the second and fourth lines
should rhyme. To help you get started, try filling in the blank in the
poem below. Choose a word that rhymes with **fun**.

Soccer

I love to play soccer.
I think it's so much fun.
I jump, I dive, I kick the ball,
But, most of all I _____!

 ░░░░░░░░░░

Name: _____ Due Date: _____

Read to Others

It is fun to read to other people. Pick a book you know well. Practice reading the first two pages aloud at home. Try to use a different voice for each new character.

When you are ready, bring your book to school. Read the first two pages to your teacher. If the teacher thinks you are ready, read the book to your class.

After you have read your two pages, ask the class what they think will happen next. Don't tell them if they are right or wrong—just tell them to read the book!

Name: _____ Due Date: _____

Read for Fun

Books are fun to read. Pick your favorite book and practice reading it aloud. Try to read using a different voice for each new character.

When you feel good about reading the book aloud, ask an adult to read with you. Take turns reading one page at a time. The adult will be surprised to hear you read so well.

Rate yourself on how well you read aloud. Circle the face that describes how you feel.

Try this activity again with another book.

Name: _____   Due Date: _____

Sum It Up

Choose a book to read with someone at home. Take turns reading pages. When you are done, write a summary of the story on this card. Tell what happens in the beginning, middle, and at the end of the story.

_____

_____

_____

_____

_____

Name: _____   Due Date: _____

All About the Book

Read a book. Then, fill out the information below. Be prepared to do a book talk in school. Use the information on this card to help you.

Title: _____

Author: _____

Illustrator: _____

Characters: _____

Setting: _____

Problem: _____

Solution: _____

Name: _____ Due Date: _____

About the Picture

Draw a picture. Then, write a story describing all of the details in the picture. Hide your picture and read your story to someone at home. Ask the person to draw a picture based on your description. Compare the pictures to see if they are alike or different. If they are very different, think of what you can add to your story to help the person draw a picture that matches your story better.

Name: _____ Due Date: _____

The Picture's Story

Draw a picture. Be sure to include characters in the picture. Next, write a story about what is happening in the picture. Give your picture to someone else and ask that person to write a story about it. Then, compare the two stories. Are the stories the same or different? Could each story fit the picture? Talk about it with someone at home.

Name: _____   Due Date: _____

Stick Puppet Fun

Choose a character from the book _____ .
Make a stick puppet of the character. Use a craft stick, paper, glue,
ribbon, buttons, glitter, and other materials to create
the puppet.

Practice telling your character's story.
Bring your puppet to school to share the
character's story with your classmates.

Name: _____   Due Date: _____

Create a Plate Puppet

Choose a character from the book _____ .
Make a plate puppet of the character. Cut a paper plate in half. Set the
two halves on top of another plate. Have an
adult help you staple the plates together around
the edges. Fold the plates in half along the cut
to form pockets for your hand. Make eyes and a
nose on the top half using markers or construction
paper and glue. Add hair and ears, too. Then, open up
the plate and add a tongue and teeth inside the mouth.

Bring your puppet to school to share with your classmates. Use the
puppet to retell the story.

Name: _____   Due Date: _____

Be an Author (Part 1)

If you could write a book, what would it be about?

_____

_____

What would you name your book?

_____

Save this card. You will use it another day.

Name: _____   Due Date: _____

Be an Author (Part 2)

If you could write a book, what characters would be in your story?

_____

_____

How old are they? _____

What do the characters look like? Draw pictures of them on the back of this card.

Save this card along with Part 1. You will use both cards again.

Name: _____ Due Date: _____

Be an Author (Part 3)

Every story has a problem and a solution. In your story, what is the problem your characters have?

_____

_____

How do they solve the problem? _____

_____

Save this card along with Parts 1 and 2. You will use the cards again.

Name: _____ Due Date: _____

Be an Author (Part 4)

Today is the big day. Use the three story cards that you have been saving to write a story. Ask an adult to review your cards with you. Then, write the story on a separate piece of lined paper.

Make a cover for your book using construction paper. Include the title of your story and your name as the author. Then, draw and color a picture on the cover.

Bring your finished book to school to share with the class.

Name: _____ Due Date: _____

A Fairy-Tale Character

Fairy tales are filled with interesting characters. Read a few fairy tales. If you could be any character from the stories you read, which one would you be and why? Write your choice and reasons below. Be ready to share your answer with your classmates.

Character: _____

Reasons Why: _____

_____

_____

Name: _____ Due Date: _____

Original Fairy Tale

After reading some well-known fairy tales, write one of your own. Think about the setting, characters, problem, and solution in your tale. What moral will your fairy tale include? Write your ideas on the back of this card to get you started. Then, write your very own tale. After you have finished your first draft, share it with your classmates. Ask them for advice to make your final story even better.

Name: _____ Due Date: _____

Make Predictions

Pick a story that you have never read before. Ask an adult to read the story with you. After you read a page or two, stop and try to guess what will happen next. Turn the page and then read some more. Was your guess right? Were you close? Try again with the next two pages.

Keep making guesses until you finish the book.

Were any of your guesses correct? _____

What surprised you most about the story? _____

_____

Name: _____ Due Date: _____

Commercial Fun

Sit down and watch a favorite TV show with your family. During the first commercial break, try to guess what will happen next on the show. Tell the others about your guess. Then, watch to see what happens.

During the next commercial break, talk with your family about what actually happened. Were your guesses close to what happened? Explain.

_____

_____

Continue making guesses until the end of the show.

Name: _____ Due Date: _____

TV Fun

Ask an adult to watch your favorite TV show with you.

When the show is over, retell the whole story in your own words.

Was this one of your favorite episodes? _____ Why or why not?

_____

_____

Draw a picture of your favorite character from the show on the back of this card. Write the character's name below your picture.

Name: _____ Due Date: _____

Movie Fun

Ask an adult to watch your favorite movie with you. When the movie is over, have the adult ask you the questions on this card. Answer the questions aloud.

1. What is the setting of the movie?
2. Who are the main characters?
3. What is the problem in the story?
4. What is the solution to the problem?
5. Why is this your favorite movie?

On the back of this card, draw your favorite scene from the movie.

Name: _____ Due Date: _____

What Time Is It?

Make your own analog clock or use a toy clock to practice telling time. First, look at the time on a digital clock. Then, see if you can move the hands on your homemade clock to show the same time. Ask someone at home to help you.

Practice telling time for different events during the day: eating breakfast, leaving for school, eating lunch, getting home from school, eating dinner, watching a favorite TV show, doing homework, going to bed, etc. Write the times you practiced on the back of this card. Be ready to show the same times again in school.

Name: _____ Due Date: _____

How Much Time Does It Take?

Find a digital or analog clock at home. Then, have someone help you answer the questions below.

How much time does it take you to:

brush your teeth? _____   take a bath? _____

do your homework? _____   eat dinner? _____

What takes the most time? _____

What takes the least time? _____

 CD-104158 Creative Homework Assignments

Name: _____ Due Date: _____

Footsteps

Use your feet to measure objects or rooms in your home. Walking heel to toe, how many steps does it take to measure each thing below?

the length of a couch   _____ steps

the length of your bed   _____ steps

the length of the living room _____ steps

the length of the kitchen   _____ steps

Measure other objects or areas with your feet. Write the measurements on the back of this card. Share your answers with your classmates.

Name: _____ Due Date: _____

Estimate Step-by-Step

Guess how many steps it will take to measure each distance below. Make your guesses. Then, walk heel to toe and count the steps to see how close each guess was.

	Guess	Count
from the front door to the kitchen	_____	_____
from the kitchen to the bathroom	_____	_____
from the bathroom to your bedroom	_____	_____
from your bedroom to the front door	_____	_____

Name: _____ Due Date: _____

String Shapes

Cut a piece of string that is about 12 inches (30 cm) long. Then, practice making different shapes with the string. Draw and label your shapes on this card.

Name: _____ Due Date: _____

The Thing About String

List 4 objects that you think are about 12 inches (30 cm) long.

Object 1: _____ ☐ longer ☐ shorter

Object 2: _____ ☐ longer ☐ shorter

Object 3: _____ ☐ longer ☐ shorter

Object 4: _____ ☐ longer ☐ shorter

Cut a 12-inch (30 cm) length of string. Compare each object to the string. Is the object longer or shorter than the string? Check the correct box. Then, circle the object that is closest to 12 inches long.

Name: _____   Due Date: _____

A Toss of the Dice

Toss a pair of dice. Then, add and subtract the numbers that you roll. Write the number sentences below. Follow the example.

Example:

___1___ + ___2___ = ___3___   ___2___ − ___1___ = ___1___

_____ + _____ = _____   _____ − _____ = _____

_____ + _____ = _____   _____ − _____ = _____

_____ + _____ = _____   _____ − _____ = _____

Name: _____   Due Date: _____

A Number Word Game

Practice saying the number words below. Write each word on a small index card and mix up the cards. Practice putting the cards in order.

one	five	nine
two	six	ten
three	seven	eleven
four	eight	twelve

Make three number sentences using your cards. Write them on the back of this card. Example: **one** + **two** = **three**.

Name: _____ Due Date: _____

Plates of Popcorn

Practice counting by tens and ones. You will need one cupful of popcorn.

1. Pour the popcorn into a bowl. Count the pieces, making as many piles of 10 as you can. Glue each set of 10 pieces to a paper plate.

2. Take the leftover pieces. Glue each one to a separate paper plate.

3. Count by tens and then ones to find the total number of pieces.

   Write your totals here: _____ tens + _____ ones = _____

Have someone check your work.

Name: _____ Due Date: _____

More Tens and Ones

Use handfuls of raisins, dry cereal, or coins to count out tens and ones. Make piles of 10 objects and set aside any leftover pieces. Count by tens and then ones to discover the total number.

Write your totals here: _____ tens + _____ ones = _____

Have someone check your work.

Name: _____ Due Date: _____

Flat Shapes

Name the shapes below.

 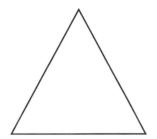 

_____ _____ _____

Now, use toothpicks and mini marshmallows to create these shapes.
Bring your marshmallow shapes to school to share with the class.

Name: _____ Due Date: _____

3-D Shapes

Use toothpicks and mini marshmallows to create the 3-D shapes below.

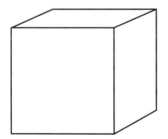 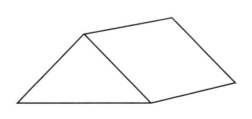 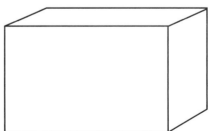

_____ _____ _____

Bring your marshmallow shapes to school to show your classmates.
Learn the names of these shapes and write them on the lines above.

Name: _____ Due Date: _____

Patterns

Each row of shapes below makes a pattern. Draw the correct shapes to continue each pattern. The first one has been done for you.

△ ○ △ ○   △ ○ △ ○

⬠ □ ⬠ □   ___ ___ ___ ___

□ △ △ □ △ △   ___ ___ ___ ___

○ ⬠ ◇ ○ ⬠ ◇   ___ ___ ___ ___

Use crayons to color the shapes, but keep the patterns the same.

Name: _____ Due Date: _____

Plenty of Patterns

Continue each pattern below.

△ △ ⬠ △ △ ⬠   ___ ___ ___ ___

◇ ○ ○ ◇ ○ ○   ___ ___ ___ ___

□ □ ⬠ △ □ □ ⬠ △   ___ ___ ___ ___

Draw two more patterns on the back of this card. Bring the card to school and give the patterns to a classmate to continue. Be ready to explain your patterns.

Name: _____ Due Date: _____

Under the Sea Counting Book (Part 1)

Make a number book filled with different sea creatures.

1. Take 10 pieces of light blue construction paper. Write a different number and sentence (see Part 2) across the top of each page.

2. Draw one picture each day for 10 days. Each picture should show what the sentence describes.

When you finish all 10 pictures, bring them to school to share with your class. Do your pictures look the same or different? Your teacher will help you put the pages together to make a counting book. Read your book with the class.

Name: _____ Due Date: _____

Under the Sea Counting Book (Part 2)

1 One octopus hides in a cave.
2 Two whales swim through the sea.
3 Three dolphins leap out of the water.
4 Four sharks dart through a sunken ship.
5 Five eels slither in the seaweed.
6 Six starfish stick to the rocks.
7 Seven sea horses float up and down.
8 Eight crabs crawl on the seafloor.
9 Nine fish swim over the coral reef.
10 Ten seashells lie in the sand.

Name: _____ Due Date: _____

Fun with Coins (Part 1)

Ask an adult for a clear, plastic or glass jar. Then, use the jar to collect pennies for one week. Put your pennies in the jar each day. At the end of the week, guess how many pennies you collected in all. Write your guess below. Next, count the pennies and write your actual total.

Guess: _____ Actual Total: _____

Keep going! Collect pennies for another week and guess again.

Guess: _____ Actual Total: _____

How much money did you collect in all? _____

Name: _____ Due Date: _____

Fun with Coins (Part 2)

Answer the questions below.

1. How many pennies equal one nickel? _____

2. How many nickels could you get for
   the pennies you collected in Part 1? _____

   How many pennies would be left over? _____

3. How many nickels equal one dime? _____

4. How many dimes could you get for your nickels? _____

   How many nickels would be left over? _____

 CD-104158 Creative Homework Assignments

Name: _____ Due Date: _____

A Dollar Bill

Ask an adult to show you a U.S. one-dollar bill. Look at the front of the bill. What do you see?

What numbers do you see? _____

What color is the bill? _____

On the back of this card, draw things that you think you could buy with one dollar.

Name: _____ Due Date: _____

One Dollar

Ask an adult to show you a U.S. one-dollar bill. Look at the back of the bill. What do you see?

What is the big word written in the middle? _____

There is also a picture of a bird on the
back of the bill. What kind of bird is it? _____

This bird is a national symbol of the United States. Draw the bird on the back of this card.

Name: _____ Due Date: _____

Hundred Necklace

Counting to 100 can be fun!

Take a piece of yarn that is at least 24 inches (61 cm) long. Tie a knot at one end of the yarn. String ring cereal onto the yarn, one piece at a time. If the cereal is multi-colored, try making patterns with the different colors. Count until you fit 100 pieces of cereal on the yarn. Then, tie the ends together to make a necklace. Wear your necklace to school to show your classmates.

Name: _____ Due Date: _____

Hundred Count

You can count to 100 in many different ways. Try counting by 2s, 5s, 10s, and 20s. Use 100 pieces of cereal to help you. As you count to 100, make piles of 2, 5, 10, or 20. Each time you count, write down how many piles it takes to make 100.

How many piles of 2 did you make? _____

How many piles of 5 did you make? _____

How many piles of 10 did you make? _____

How many piles of 20 did you make? _____

Name: _____ Due Date: _____

Symmetry

Draw the right side of the butterfly to match the left side shown.

Draw another butterfly on the back of this card. Color only one side. Let a classmate color the other side to match yours.

Name: _____ Due Date: _____

More Symmetry

Draw the missing half of each picture below so that both sides match.

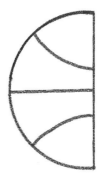

Draw half of a picture for someone to finish on the back of this card. Bring it to school and trade with a classmate.

Name: _____ Due Date: _____

Counting Candies (Part 1)

Open a bag of candy-covered chocolates, such as M&M's®, and pour them onto a table. Sort the candies into piles by color. Use tally marks to count how many of each color there are.

Example: red ____~~HHl~~ ll____ = __7__

blue _____ = _____   orange _____ = _____

brown _____ = _____   red _____ = _____

green _____ = _____   yellow _____ = _____

Name: _____ Due Date: _____

Counting Candies (Part 2)

Use your tally marks from Part 1 to color in the graph below. In each row, color one block for every piece of candy you counted. Use a different color for each row to match the candies.

blue																			
brown																			
green																			
orange																			
red																			
yellow																			

 CD-104158 Creative Homework Assignments

Name: _____ Due Date: _____

Sock Match

Help with the laundry by finding socks that match. Fold each pair of matching socks together.

1. How many pairs of socks did you match in all? _____

2. Were there any socks without a match? _____

   If yes, how many? _____

Next, put the socks into groups. Make one group for each person in your family. Take each group of socks to the right room.

Name: _____ Due Date: _____

Sock Puppet

Ask an adult for a sock that you can use to make a puppet. To make your puppet, decorate the sock using glue, buttons, ribbon, fabric scraps, colorful paper, and other materials. Decorate your puppet with lots of geometric shapes. Use at least four different shapes.

Take a close look at your finished sock puppet. Then, answer these questions on the back of this card: What shapes did you use? Are some of the shapes congruent? Are some similar? Is your puppet symmetrical?

Give your puppet a name and bring it to school. Be ready to name and describe the different shapes you used to create the puppet.

Name: _____ Due Date: _____

Go Shopping

Bring this card with you the next time you go to the grocery store. Find two items that you would like to buy. Write the name and price of each item. Then, add the two prices together. How much would it cost to buy the two items? Do the math below.

Items: _____ Price: _____

_____ + _____

Total: _____

Name: _____ Due Date: _____

Compare Costs

Bring this card and a pencil the next time you go to the grocery store. Then, compare costs of your favorite cereals in the cereal aisle.

Look at the weight of each box before you compare prices. (The weight is usually listed on the front of the box near the bottom.) Be sure to compare the prices of equal-sized boxes.

List the cereal names and prices on the back of this card. Circle the most expensive cereal with red. Circle the least expensive cereal with blue. Back at home, list the cereals in order of price on another sheet of paper. Bring this card and your list to share with the class.

Name: _____ Due Date: _____

A Math Story

Mr. Rodriguez went to the grocery store. He bought a dozen eggs, a package of 6 granola bars, 2 chickens, a gallon of milk, a bag of 6 hard rolls, a box of 12 ice-cream bars, and 2 six-packs of juice boxes.

How many **individual** items did Mr. Rodriguez buy? _____
(Hint: If your answer is 9, try again.)

Show your work on the back of this card. Then, write sentences to tell how you found the answer.

Use lined paper to make your own grocery list. Ask a classmate to count the individual items.

Name: _____ Due Date: _____

Another Math Story

Mrs. Burns went to the hardware store. She bought a dozen rags, a bag of 6 sponges, 2 boxes of 6 light bulbs each, 2 packages of 50 screws each, a box of 24 washers, and 3 six-packs of toilet paper.

How many **individual** items did Mrs. Burns buy? _____
(Hint: If your answer is 10, try again.)

Show your work on the back of this card. Then, write sentences to tell how you found the answer.

Use lined paper to make your own shopping list. Ask a classmate to count the individual items.

Name: _____ Due Date: _____

Fun with a Calculator

Write each number in standard form on the first line. Then, enter the number into a calculator. Turn the calculator upside down and read the word it forms. Write the word on the second line to finish each phrase.

A. 300 + 30 + 8 = _____   buzzing _____

B. 7,000 + 700 + 30 + 8 = _____   school _____

C. 3,000 + 700 + 4 = _____   black _____

D. 30,000 + 5,000 + 6 = _____   Canada _____

E. 70,000 + 7,000 + 300 + 40 + 5 = _____   snail _____

Name: _____ Due Date: _____

More Calculator Fun

The numbers 0–9 look like letters when read upside down on a calculator:

0 = O   1 = I   2 = Z   3 = E   4 = h   5 = S   6 = g   7 = L   8 = B   9 = G

Make a word using some of these letters. _____

What number spells that word when read upside down? _____

Now, write a short riddle to go with your word. Then, write a number sentence whose answer is that number, too.

    Example: What is yellow and black and likes flowers?
        300 + 38 = _____   (Answer: a bee, or 338)

Name: _____ Due Date: _____

Cereal Sets

Place 2 pieces of cereal in a group. Then, make 2 more groups of 2. How many pieces of cereal do you have in all? Draw the groups below. Then, write the number sentence.

_____ × _____ = _____

Try again with groups of 3 pieces of cereal each, then 4 pieces each. Draw the groups and write each number sentence below.

_____ × _____ = _____

_____ × _____ = _____

Name: _____ Due Date: _____

Multiplication Deck

Take a deck of playing cards. Remove all of the face cards so that only the aces and number cards remain. Shuffle the cards that are left and put them facedown in a stack.

Turn over the top two cards. Multiply the two numbers. (An ace stands for the number 1.) Write the number sentence below. Play again.

_____ × _____ = _____   _____ × _____ = _____

_____ × _____ = _____   _____ × _____ = _____

_____ × _____ = _____   _____ × _____ = _____

Name: _____ Due Date: _____

The Great Divide

Count the total number of dots.
Write your total in the first box.

$$\boxed{} \div \boxed{3} = \boxed{}$$

Using a pencil, circle groups of 3 dots
each. How many groups can you make?
Write your answer in the last box above.

• • • • •

• • • • •

Erase your pencil marks and start again.
This time, circle groups of 5 dots each.
How many groups can you make? Fill in the
boxes to complete the number sentence.

• • • • •

$$\boxed{} \div \boxed{5} = \boxed{}$$

Name: _____ Due Date: _____

Divide and Conquer

Make a pile with 24 pieces of cereal. Then, divide the cereal into groups
of 2 pieces each.

How many groups do you have in all? _____ Draw the groups below.

Now, finish the number sentence: __24__ ÷ __2__ = _____

Try again, this time dividing the cereal into groups of 3 pieces each.
Show your work on the back of this card.

 CD-104158 Creative Homework Assignments

Name: _____ Due Date: _____

Fraction Snack

Ask an adult to help you make some snacks. You will need 4 tortillas or 4 square pieces of bread. Use the tortillas or bread to make 2 of your favorite kind of quesadilla or sandwich. Do not cut your snacks yet. Draw a picture of your snacks on the back of this card.

Cut your first snack in half.
Draw the cut line on your picture. Color $\frac{1}{2}$ yellow.

Cut the other snack into fourths.
Draw the cut lines on your picture. Color $\frac{1}{4}$ blue.

Enjoy your snacks with the adult who helped you make them.

Name: _____ Due Date: _____

Pretzel Puzzle

Count out 12 mini pretzels. Line them up on a table as shown here:

Take away $\frac{1}{4}$ of the pretzels. How many are left? _____

Take away $\frac{1}{3}$ of the remaining pretzels. How many are left? _____

Take away $\frac{1}{2}$ of the remaining pretzels. How many are left? _____

Enjoy the pretzels as a snack.

Name: _____ Due Date: _____

Tree House

Draw insects and other animals that live in trees on the tree below.
List their names on the back of this card.

Name: _____ Due Date: _____

Winter Sleep

Draw an animal that sleeps or hibernates in winter on the back of this
card. Think of a good reason for the animal to wake up. Be prepared to
tell your story to your classmates.

 CD-104158 Creative Homework Assignments

Name: _____ Due Date: _____

Animals We Know

Think about the animals that live in your neighborhood or area. Draw a picture showing animals that live above the ground, on the ground, and underground. Be ready to describe the animals in your picture to the class.

Name: _____ Due Date: _____

What Animals Eat

Look at the animals in the picture below. Do you know what each animal eats? A **carnivore** eats only meat. An **herbivore** eats only plants. Color the carnivores pink. Color the herbivores green. Label each animal.

Name: _____ Due Date: _____

Predators

Many animals are predators. A **predator** is an animal that hunts other animals for food. List four predators on this card. Then, name some of the animals each predator hunts for food.

1. _____

2. _____

3. _____

4. _____

Choose one predator to draw on the back of this card.

Name: _____ Due Date: _____

Prey

Animals that are hunted by other animals for food are called **prey**. Both large and small animals can be prey to other animals. A predator may also be the prey of another predator. List four examples of prey below. Then, choose one example of prey and draw it on the back of this card.

1. _____

2. _____

3. _____

4. _____

Name: _____   Due Date: _____

Extinct Animals

An extinct animal is an animal that no longer exists on Earth. Animals become extinct for many reasons. Do some research. Find an animal that is extinct. Then, answer the questions below.

1. What is the name of the animal?
2. Where did the animal live?
3. How do scientists think the animal became extinct?
4. Can you find any other interesting information about this animal?

Use the back of this card to write your answers in a paragraph. On another sheet of paper, draw a picture of the animal.

Name: _____   Due Date: _____

Endangered Animals

Some animals are on the endangered species list. This means that the animals are in danger of becoming extinct. Do some research. Find an animal that is endangered. Then, answer the questions below.

1. What is the name of the animal?
2. Where does the animal live?
3. Why is the animal endangered?
4. Is there anything humans can do to help save this animal from extinction?

Using what you have learned, make a plan to help save this animal. Write your plan on the back of this card.

Name: _____   Due Date: _____

Recycling Paper

Paper is made from trees. Think about all of the paper your school uses each day. To help save the world's forests, think of ways that you can save or reuse paper. This is called **conserving** and **recycling**. Use this card to make a list of different ways to conserve and recycle paper.

_____

_____

_____

Back at school, work with your class to generate ideas for conserving and recycling in your school. Present your plan to the school principal.

Name: _____   Due Date: _____

Don't Be a Litterbug!

It is important to keep our world clean. How can you convince people to stop littering in your neighborhood? Make a list of your ideas on this card. Be ready to share your ideas with your classmates.

_____

_____

_____

Pick your favorite idea. Then, figure out a way to put it into action. Be sure to report back to the class if your plan is a success.

Name: _____ Due Date: _____

Using Water

All living things need water to live. People use water for many different purposes. Think about all of the ways you use water each day. Make a list on the back of this card.

Next, keep track of the ways you use water for one week. Write down how and when you use the water each time. At the end of the week, review your notes. Did you use water in any ways not listed on the back of this card? If so, add them to your list.

What was the most surprising or unexpected way you used water?

_____

Name: _____ Due Date: _____

Saving Water

People need clean water to live. Think of different ways to save water. Make a list on the back of this card.

How many ways did you think of to conserve water? _____
Compare lists with your classmates.

Next, take your favorite idea for conserving water and act on it at home for one week. Ask others at home to help out, too. At the end of the week, think about the changes you made. Was it hard or easy for you to make those changes? Be ready to discuss your experience with the class.

Name: _____ Due Date: _____

Color Fun with Pasta

Ask an adult to help you dye some pasta. Use only red, yellow, and blue food coloring to make six different colors in all. On the back of this card, explain how you can make orange, green, and purple pasta, too. To make each color, put some dry pasta in a resealable plastic bag. Add a few drops of food coloring and water. Seal the bag and shake it. Spread the colorful pasta on paper towels and let dry for at least one day.

After your pasta is dry, use it to make a picture. Be sure to include all six colors in your picture. First, draw your picture with glue on a sheet of construction paper. Then, place the colorful pasta on top of the glue. Bring your picture to school and show it to the class.

Name: _____ Due Date: _____

Colors of Nature

Think of a color. Write the name of the color here: _____.
Draw three things found in nature that are this color.

Bring your card to school and tell your classmates what pictures you drew. Keep your card hidden and see if they can guess the color. Then, show them your pictures to reveal your secret color.

Name: _____ Due Date: _____

Colors of a Rainbow

There are seven colors in a rainbow. The colors always appear in the same order. Remember the name **Roy G. Biv** to learn the order. Each letter in the name starts a different color word. **R** is for red, **O** is for orange, and so on. Can you guess what colors the other letters stand for? Ask an adult to help you learn the name of each color in a rainbow.

Next, draw a rainbow on the back of this card. Be sure to include seven stripes. Then, starting with "red" on top, write the correct color word in each stripe of the rainbow. Finally, color the rainbow.

Name: _____ Due Date: _____

Fun Outside

Draw things you can do outside on a sunny day on the left. Draw things you can do outside on a windy day on the right.

Sunny Day	Windy Day

Name: _____ Due Date: _____

What to Wear?

Use eight large index cards to make a weather book.

1. Staple the cards together at the top left corners. Write "My Weather Book" on the first page (the cover). Decorate the cover.

2. Write one day of the week at the top of each page in the book. For one week, watch TV each night to see the weather forecast for the next day. Write the prediction for the day in your book. Then, go to your room and pick out an outfit to wear the next day.

3. The following night, reflect on your choice of outfit. Be ready to explain to an adult why it was a good choice or a bad choice.

Name: _____ Due Date: _____

Changes in the Weather

In some parts of the world, the weather stays the same year-round. In other places, the weather changes with each new season. Listed below are three temperatures. Under each temperature, list one activity you could do outside. On a separate piece of paper, write a paragraph about each activity.

26° Fahrenheit (-3° Celsius)	72° Fahrenheit (22° Celsius)	98° Fahrenheit (37° Celsius)
_____	_____	_____
_____	_____	_____

Name: _____ Due Date: _____

The Snowman's Letter

What would a snowman say to the sun? Pretend to be a snowman and write a letter to the sun. Plan your letter in the space below. Then, use a separate piece of paper to write the letter. Be sure that your letter includes the date, a greeting, a body, and a closing.

_____

_____

_____

_____

Name: _____ Due Date: _____

The Sun's Reply

Pretend you are the sun. You have just received a letter from a snowman asking you not to shine anymore because he is melting. Write a letter to the snowman explaining why you (the sun) are so important. Plan your letter on the front and back of this card. Then, use a separate piece of paper to write the letter. Be sure that your letter includes the date, a greeting, a body, and a closing.

_____

_____

_____

Name: _____ Due Date: _____

It's Melting!

Ask an adult for an ice cube and a bowl. How long do you think it will take for the ice cube to melt? Write your guess on the first line below.

Guess: _____ Actual Time: _____

Place the ice cube in the bowl and let it sit. Check the bowl often, keeping track of the time. How long does it take to melt completely? Write the actual time on the second line above.

How close was your guess? _____

Think of a way to speed up the melting process and try again. Draw a picture of your idea and record your results on the back of this card.

Name: _____ Due Date: _____

An Icy Experiment

What do you think takes longer: melting or freezing an ice cube?

Write your guess here: _____
Then, ask an adult to help you try this experiment.

1. Take an ice-cube tray out of the freezer. Remove one ice cube and put it in a bowl. Fill the empty space in the tray with water. Then, put the tray back in the freezer.
2. Record your start time on the back of this card. Check the bowl and tray often to see which is done first. Record each finish time.
3. Describe your results on the back of this card. Was your guess correct? What factors could have affected the outcome?

Name: _____ Due Date: _____

Kitchen Sounds

You can hear many sounds in a kitchen. Stay very quiet and listen for sounds in your own kitchen. Can you hear water running, the toaster popping, or a timer ticking?

Write the sounds that you hear on this card. Share your answers with your classmates. Did you hear the same sounds or different ones?

_____

_____

_____

Name: _____ Due Date: _____

Kitchen Smells

What can you smell in your kitchen at dinnertime? On the back of this card, draw and label the things that you smell. Bring your card to school to share with the class.

Name: _____ Due Date: _____

Be Healthy

Good health is important. Eating right, getting enough sleep, and exercising every day will help you do your very best in school and in any sport you play.

Use the paper provided by your teacher to create a poster of things that keep you healthy. Include words and pictures, and make your poster as colorful as you can.

Name: _____ Due Date: _____

Eating Healthy

Eating food that is good for you is not always easy to do. When you are hungry, sometimes it is easier to grab a bag of chips or a few cookies than it is to make a healthy snack. The trick is to always have healthy foods at your fingertips.

Find a healthy recipe for a quick snack by doing some research or talking to an adult. (You might try looking on cereal boxes or other healthy food labels for ideas, too.)

On your assigned day, bring your recipe to class, along with samples of your healthy treat to share.

Name: _____ Due Date: _____

Signs on the Street

Watch for traffic signs on your way to school and on your way home. Choose two signs and draw them on the back of this card. Then, make big signs for the classroom using construction paper, glue, and markers.

Think about what the signs mean and why they are important. What might happen if the signs were not there?

_____

_____

_____

Name: _____ Due Date: _____

Safety Tip of the Day

Adults are always telling you things that you should do to keep yourself safe. Talk to an adult at home and pick a safety tip to share with the whole class.

Draw a picture of your safety tip on the back of this card. Be prepared to explain your tip to the class on your assigned day.

Name: _____ Due Date: _____

What I Like

Look through old magazines and cut out pictures of things you like. The pictures can be of favorite animals, clothes, toys, places, or other things. Cut out pictures that you think will help others learn more about you. Glue the pictures onto construction paper to make a collage. Bring your collage to school and share it with your classmates.

Name: _____ Due Date: _____

What I Like About Me

List three things you like best about yourself. Think about the things you can do (Example: I can run fast.), the kind of person you are (Example: I am friendly.), or the way you look (Example: I have freckles.).

1. _____

2. _____

3. _____

On the back of this card, draw a special picture frame. Then, glue a photograph or draw a picture of yourself inside the frame.

Name: _____ Due Date: _____

An Interview

Think of a relative or other adult you admire. Ask a parent or guardian to help you set up an interview with that person. Use the questions below for your interview or make up your own questions.

What is your name?   Do you have children?
What is your job?   Do you have pets?
Do you have any hobbies?   Can you speak a second language?
What is your favorite color?   Do you like to travel?

Take notes during your interview. Later, use your notes to write a paragraph about the person. Draw a picture of the person, too.

Name: _____ Due Date: _____

Saving Money

It's never too early to learn how to save money. Think of different ways you can earn and save money. Some children earn an allowance for doing chores at home. Some save change from their lunch money. What other ways can you think of to save money? Make a list on the back of this card.

Start saving money now. On another piece of paper, write a simple plan for how you can earn and save money. Then, describe what you will do with the money you save. Use a piggy bank or jar to collect the money you save. Once a week, count your money and keep a log.

Name: _____ Due Date: _____

Independence Day

Many countries celebrate their own Independence Day. It is a day that symbolizes freedom. The United States celebrates its Independence Day on July 4. On that day, U.S. flags are flown everywhere in celebration.

Draw and color a U.S. flag on the back of this card. Look at a picture or an actual flag as a reference. Then, use the library to find out two facts about the flag. Write these facts on the lines below. Be ready to share your facts with the class.

1. _____

2. _____

Name: _____ Due Date: _____

An American Indian Outfit

Have an adult help you make an American Indian vest and headband. Fold a paper grocery bag flat and turn it upside down. Cut a half circle from the top edge and one from each side to create a neck hole and two armholes. Cut a slit down the center of the bag (through the front only) from the center hole to the large opening of the bag. Cut a strip from the bottom of the vest to make the headband. Decorate your vest and headband with feathers and American Indian symbols.

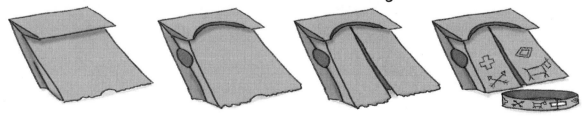

Name: _____   Due Date: _____

Transportation

On a blank piece of paper, draw a car, boat, and other things that help you travel. Cut out your pictures. Then, write the words "Air," "Land," and "Water" on three small index cards. Use the cards to help you sort the pictures into categories.

When you are done, store your cards and pictures in resealable plastic bags. Use a separate bag for each category. Bring your bags to school to share with the class.

Name: _____   Due Date: _____

My Dream-Mobile

Design a dream-mobile. It can be something that moves on land, goes in or on the water, or flies through the sky. Draw your dream-mobile on this card and bring it to school to show your classmates. Be ready to tell about the special features of your dream-mobile.

Name: _____ Due Date: _____

Community Volunteers

There are many workers who help make a community a great place to live. Some of these workers are volunteers who donate their time. Think about how you can help make your community a better place. Make a list of jobs that you and your friends could do to help.

_____

_____

_____

Circle your favorite idea. Then, ask your parent or guardian to help you act on it.

Name: _____ Due Date: _____

Laws in Your Community

Many laws are different from community to community. In some places, people must wear helmets when riding bikes. In other places, young people have to be home by a certain hour at night. Think about your own community. Talk to an adult. Ask about the laws in your community.

Write one of your community's laws on the back of this card. Tell if you agree or disagree with the law and why.

Is there a law that you think your community should have but does not? With an adult's help, write a letter to the editor of your local newspaper. Explain your idea for this law and why you think it is important.

Name: _____ Due Date: _____

I Live Here

Draw three rings on a paper plate. Then, follow the directions below to pinpoint where you live.

1. On the outer ring, write the name of the continent on which you live.
2. On the middle ring, write the name of the country in which you live.
3. On the inner ring, write the name of the state or province in which you live.
4. In the center, write the name of the town or city in which you live.

Color your plate with light colors when you are done.

Name: _____ Due Date: _____

Oceans Around Me

Use your social studies textbook, an atlas, or an encyclopedia to research the oceans that surround your country or continent. Draw an outline of your country on a piece of construction paper. Fill in the outline of the continent around it. Then, write the names of the oceans that border the continent. Color the oceans blue. Draw a smiley face on the map where you live.

Name: _____ Due Date: _____

National Symbols

There are many symbols that can represent a country. Learn about your country's national symbols. List some of them below. Then, use construction paper to draw, color, and label those symbols.

1. national flag _____

2. national bird _____

3. national flower _____

4. national anthem _____

5. other: _____

Name: _____ Due Date: _____

My Flag

A country like the United States of America has many symbols that represent it. There is the flag, the bald eagle, the Great Seal, and the national anthem. Each symbol tells something about the country.

Think about yourself and your family. What kinds of symbols would best represent you?

Using construction paper, create a flag that would tell others about you and your family. Be ready to describe what the different parts of the flag stand for.

Name: _____ Due Date: _____

The President

The president of the United States is a busy person with many different jobs to do. What do you think those jobs include? Write your ideas below.

_____

_____

_____

_____

Next, do some research to learn what the president's jobs actually are. List them on the back of this card. Circle the jobs you guessed correctly.

Name: _____ Due Date: _____

If I Were President

Imagine that you are the president or leader of your country. What five things would you do to make the world a better place? Answer on the lines below. Use the back of this card if you need more room.

1. _____

2. _____

3. _____

4. _____

5. _____

Name: _____ Due Date: _____

What Can You Say?

If you speak more than one language, think about a word or phrase you would like to teach the class. If you speak only English, ask your parents for help in looking up some foreign words. Then, choose one word or phrase to teach your classmates.

Write the foreign word or phrase on the line below. Write the definition in English on the back of this card.

_____

Bring this card to school and teach your classmates the new word or phrase.

Name: _____ Due Date: _____

Traditions

We all have traditions that we repeat every year at the same time. Talk to your parents or grandparents about the special things your family does on different holidays.

On the back of this card, draw a picture of you or your family doing one of these special things. Be prepared to share your family's tradition with the class. If possible, bring in some special items related to the tradition to show your classmates.

Name: _____ Due Date: _____

A Monthly Schedule

Sometimes, it is wise to schedule ahead for an entire month. That way, you can keep track of important assignments, play dates, school events, and after-school activities.

Practice using a monthly calendar to record your own schedule of events. Ask your teacher and someone at home to help you.

Name: _____ Due Date: _____

Weekly Schedule

Tell about one thing you do on each day of the week.

Sunday _____

Monday _____

Tuesday _____

Wednesday _____

Thursday _____

Friday _____

Saturday _____

Name: _____ Due Date: _____

Uh-Oh Moments

Talk to someone at home about the following situations:

- You know that a classmate is stealing things from the classroom.

- Another classmate is asking you for answers on a test.

- Another student keeps threatening you at recess time.

- Someone in your class is calling you names.

What should you do? Be ready to share your thoughts with your teacher or classmates.

Name: _____ Due Date: _____

Mistakes Happen

Have you ever made a mistake and felt awful afterward? Have you ever made the same mistake again? Think of a mistake that you have made. Write it down on the back of this card. Then, think of at least one thing you have learned from that mistake.

Be prepared to share your information with the teacher. He or she might be able to help you learn more from your experience.

Remember that mistakes happen. The important thing is to learn from your mistakes so that you can make better choices in the future.

 CD-104158 Creative Homework Assignments

Name: _____ Due Date: _____

Making Good Decisions

Sometimes, you have to make quick decisions all by yourself. Being prepared and knowing what to do in certain situations can help you make good decisions.

Read the problem below. Think about it carefully. Then, on the back of this card, list three things you could do to help solve the problem. Discuss your ideas with adults at home to see if they agree or disagree.

Problem: On your way home from school, you meet a woman who is crying. She says she has lost her new puppy. Then, she asks you to take just a few minutes to help her find it.

Name: _____ Due Date: _____

Seeking Advice

When you have a problem, it can be helpful to ask others for advice. The next time you have a problem, write it down and bring it to school to put in the advice box. You do not have to put your name on the paper. If it is a personal problem that you would like to discuss with your teacher or counselor privately, put your name on the card along with this request.

Each week, your teacher will choose some of the problems to read to the class. Then, you and your classmates will get a chance to come up with advice or solutions.

Name: _____ Due Date: _____

Building Character

Do you know what it means when someone says a person has good character? Think about the following words: **trustworthiness, kindness, honesty, responsibility, fairness,** and **citizenship**. These words are called character traits.

Choose three of these traits. On a separate piece of paper, define the traits in your own words. Then, look up the words in a dictionary. How close were you to understanding their true definitions? Discuss these words with someone at home. Draw a picture for one of the words that shows its real meaning. Bring your picture to school. Ask the class to guess which trait the picture shows.

Name: _____ Due Date: _____

Taking Chances

Think of something you would like to learn to do, even if you are not sure that you can succeed at it. It can be something like playing the piano or riding a unicycle. After you have picked a challenge, write a plan for how you can succeed. Identify the steps you will need to take to be successful. This plan, along with perseverance, can help you reach your goal.